The Lighthouse Leadership Principle

THE FIVE SECRETS TO

GROWING

&

GUIDING

PEOPLE

PETE WALKEY

First published by Dog Ear Publishing
4010 W. 86th Street, Ste H
Indianapolis, IN 46268
www.dogearpublishing.net

ISBN: 1-59858-073-6
Library of Congress Control Number: 2005934561

This book is printed on acid-free paper.

Printed in the United States of America

To my wife Jill

You are the greatest earthly treasure God has given me.

You make me want to be a better leader.

Contents

Acknowledgements

God: Thank you for your unconditional love, the gift of eternal salvation, and the leading and guiding of this book. Thank you for the millions of blessings you have poured out on our family.

Jill: Thank you for loving me with all of my flaws. You're the most beautiful woman on this planet, and the wisest woman I know. You're the greatest earthly gift God has given me, and someday I hope to grow into the lighthouse God intended you to have as a husband.

Kaylee: Daddy loves you Kaylee Waylee, and is so proud of the precious princess you've become. Thank you for loving me and laughing with me. I love you bigger than the house. God has all the answers.

Ellie: Daddy loves you Ellie Bell, and is so proud of the beautiful flower you've blossomed into. Thank you for loving me and believing in me. I love you bigger than the house. God knows all.

Kylie: Daddy loves you Kylie Wylie, and is so proud of the bright and shiny jewel you've grown into. Thank you for telling me that you love me at the exact time I need to hear it. I love you bigger than the house. God sees, hears and knows all.

Bill and Tara Morris: Thank you for being the blessings you've been to our family. We love you and now understand the meaning of Godly friends. You have a beautiful family and we're grateful to know you the way we do.

Eldon Kibbey: Thank you for spending every Thursday with me for the past couple of years. Thanks for teaching me about God, leadership, relationships, community, and what it means to be a Godly businessman. Thanks for being a true mentor. Jill and I are grateful that you and Sandy are in our lives. We love you.

Thanks to Ryan Mackowiak for your graphic design genius branding this book series, the cover and all the visual pieces of the Lighthouse pie. I don't know how you do it, but it is brilliant. Thanks for being a friend. Thanks to the Lighthouse Leadership Group board of directors; Eldon Kibbey, Mark Canada, Bill Morris, Andrew Lockerbie, and Ryan Mack. Thanks for your support and love: Mom, Dad, Linda, Dick, Dorris, Grandma Ackerman, Missy, Jeff, Trisha, Cyndi, Jeff Seward, Mike Porter, and Bill Goodrich.

Preface

Every person you know is experiencing stress in at least one of the five main storms of life: *Money, Marriage, Job, Health or Family.*

Consider these alarming statistics:

- 75% of people would quit their job if they won the lottery
- 70% of doctor visits are stress-related
- 65% of Americans are overweight
- 50% of marriages end in divorce
- 80% of divorces cite money as the #1 cause

Included in these stats are people in your family, your neighborhood and your organization. This information gives you "eyes" to see them as delicate humans, rather than machines, as you lead and guide them to extraordinary results. Do you desire to be the lighthouse people want to be guided by? Do you want to be the leader people want to follow? The secret is found in *The Lighthouse Leadership Principle.*

In this book you will discover the five secrets to growing and guiding people. You can apply these secrets to both your work and your family life. If you follow this simple formula, you will influence the people in your sphere of interaction in a way you never could have imagined. The secret unfolds with the story of the lighthouse.

Chapter 1
The Story of the Lighthouse

Have you ever been called into your boss's office unexpectedly? You can imagine my curiosity when I got the call. The short walk down the hallway seemed like a mile. Each step closer produced another fearful thought. My heart raced so fast, I thought it was going to explode. When he asked me to shut the door, I knew it wasn't good.

Soon after he began talking I interrupted and asked, "Are you firing me?" He said yes, and began explaining. He must have talked another twenty minutes, but I didn't hear a word. My mind filled with fear: What will I tell my wife and three kids? How will I pay my bills? How could I find a job over the holidays?

During the drive home I reflected on a ten-year career in corporate America. Hurt from being fired, but relieved I didn't have to go back the next day.

This began a two-year process of soul searching. People started asking me questions like:

- What would you love to do for a living?
- What kind of people would you love to work with?
- If you could create your perfect working environment, what would it look like?

I realized that after a decade of climbing the corporate ladder, it was leaning against the wrong tree. I had been pursuing awards and recognition more than relationships and purpose. I was "me" focused rather than being "people" focused. I became the person who was pretending to be happy and "successful", but was actually miserable.

This book is for people who want to be more effective leaders at work and at home. For people who want more influence with the people in their sphere of interaction. This book is for people searching for the secret to a more fulfilling life. That secret is found in the story of the lighthouse.

The Story of the Lighthouse

How many lighthouses are there in the world? What about in the United States? There are 50,000 lighthouses in the world and 1,500 in the U.S. Can you guess the state with the most lighthouses? If you guessed Florida or Maine you would be wrong. The state with the most is Michigan, with 312.

In order to endure harsh weather conditions, like powerful waves, piercing rain and violent storms, lighthouses must be built on a **Rock Solid Foundation**. To withstand the storms of life, every person must also have a strong foundation, built on relationships. The right ones, and in the right priority.

Guess how many of the 50,000 lighthouses are exactly alike? A good sea captain knows that *none* of the 50,000 lighthouses in the world are exactly alike. They differ in size, shape, and color. They send out different flashes of light. Their foghorns have different sound patterns, and some even transmit radio signals. They call this its *Unique Character*.

You also have a unique character. There was and never will be a person born that is exactly like you. Your fingerprints are unique. The sound of your voice, speech pattern and words you choose are unique to you. Your likes, dislikes, strengths and weaknesses all make up the total package with your name on it.

Every employee you lead has a unique character. It's the sum total of their skills, abilities, desires and past experiences. It's what they do for fun and what makes them laugh.

Lighthouses don't try to be all things to all people. You probably never saw a lighthouse trying to be a streetlight or porch light. They stand tall and shine their light. They *Know Their Purpose*. Could you imagine if a lighthouse tried to take on other responsibilities, and wasn't there for a ship during a stormy night? It would be disaster.

The same is true with you. God made you for a purpose. You were born to do big things with your life. God gave you interests, skills, abilities, strengths, and desires. He "wired" you a certain way before you were born. He already gave you everything you need to fulfill your purpose on this earth. You will experience the most success and fulfillment when you discover and live your purpose.

God made you a leader for a purpose. He put you in your organization, your family, your neighborhood, and your circle of friends for a specific purpose. You will experience more success, fulfillment and satisfaction as a leader, when you discover what God's purpose is for you in the lives of the people you are leading.

Before lighthouses became totally automated, a "keeper" had to perform daily tasks to keep it running smoothly. His daily duties included cleaning the glass from the rain, salt water, and other impurities that would hamper the beacon. When the dirt was removed, the maximum light would shine brightly in order to ***Attract*** ships to shore.

The same is true with you. If your "glass", or personality, is "dirty", it will hinder your light from shining. It will reduce your ability to attract people. Negative comments, interrupting people, or talking too much are examples of "dirt". These things need to be cleaned so your beacon can shine brightly. When you have an attractive personality, people want to be around you.

When you are maximizing your attractiveness as leader, people are drawn to you like bugs to a bug light. People are inspired and motivated by people with attractive personalities.

Once the lighthouse is shining brightly it can attract and ***Guide*** ships into the harbor. It influences the path of the ships, and leads them to safety.

You are the same way. When you have an attractive personality people will give you permission to guide them. It's much easier to influence people when they are drawn to you, and want to be led by you, than if you try to "throw your weight" and use your authority to get things done. Leading is much more fun when we focus on *attracting* people rather than *convincing* them to follow us.

Are you ready to discover the five secrets to growing and guiding your people?

> *You are the light of the world. A city on a hill cannot be hidden. Neither do people light a lamp and put it under a bowl. Instead they put it on its stand, and it gives light to everyone in the house. In the same way, let your light shine before men, that they may see your good deeds and praise your Father in heaven.*

—Matthew 5:14–16

ROCK SOLID FOUNDATION

Chapter 2
Building Your Rock Solid Foundation

Because lighthouses must endure harsh weather conditions, like piercing rain, high winds, and sometimes hurricanes, they must be built on a rock solid foundation. Imagine what would happen if they were built upon sand. This is like the story of the wise and foolish builders:

Wise and Foolish Builders

Therefore everyone who hears these words of mine and puts them into practice is like a wise man who built his house on the rock. The rain came down, the streams rose, and the winds blew and beat against that house; yet it did not fall, because it had its foundation on the rock. But everyone who hears these words of mine and does not put them into practice is like a foolish man who built his house on sand. The rain came down, the streams rose, and the winds blew and beat against that house, and it fell with a great crash.

—Matthew 7:24–27

In order to survive the storms of life, you also must be built on a rock solid foundation, which is made of your relationships. The stronger your relationships, the stronger your foundation. The stronger your foundation, the more you can withstand whatever life throws at you.

Life is all About Relationships

My mom and I were eating breakfast one morning during my senior year of college. We were talking about upcoming interviews with potential employers, and she sensed I was nervous about my grades. She said that during interviews, employers look for positive attitudes, a willingness to learn, and the ability to work well with others. More importantly they look for your ability to build and grow relationships. She said life is all about relationships.

Think of the most influential people in your sphere of interaction. What is the common thread? Are they good at developing and growing relationships?

Looking at Your Personal Relationships

Let me ask you a question. What are the five most important relationships in your life? If you have more than one child or parent, you can list them as one relationship, like "children" or "parents", unless you truly value them at different levels.

Example:

1. _____ 1. Jake, Ryan, Will (Kids)

2. _____ 2. Bill (Husband)

3. _____ 3. Parents

4. _____ 4. Allison (best friend)

5. _____ 5. God

It's been said that to find a person's priorities, look where they spend their time and money. Let's see where you have been spending your time over the last week to see if we can discover any opportunities for increased fulfillment.

How much time did you spend each day, on average, with the following people?

Friends   _____

Kids   _____

Spouse   _____

God   _____

Other   _____

Any observations? Did you spend your time according to the way you planned it, or the way it just happened?

Let's take it a step further. If you could spend your time exactly as you wanted, how many hours would you spend each day, with each person?

Kids   _____

Spouse   _____

Friends   _____

God   _____

Other   _____

What conclusions do you draw from this exercise? Are you building your foundation of personal relationships on the sand or on the rock? Are you spending too much time at work and not enough time with the people in your family? If you have a weak foundation at home, it will negatively effect your performance at work. You can't be an effective spouse, parent, friend, or leader if your foundation is built on the sand.

If you're not feeling totally fulfilled, you have a great opportunity to experience more peace, joy and happiness by adjusting the time you spend with the people in your life.

Right Relationships, Right Priority

As I travel around the country speaking to audiences, people want to talk about balancing the activities and people in their lives. They want to discuss how to manage relationships among work, friends and hobbies, before talking about the relationships closest to them. They don't realize that if you're married with children, God designed you to experience 90% of your peace, joy, and happiness through your relationships with Him, your spouse, and your children.

If they would stop focusing on building their *Rolodex* and start focusing on building these relationships, they would be much more fulfilled.

I spent ten years pursuing "success" in business, hoping to find peace, joy and happiness. God showed me how to get all this and more, by focusing on building the right relationships, in the right priority. First building a relationship with Him, then with my wife Jill, and then our three daughters.

He showed me that if I spend more time with our daughters, than with Jill, we get out of balance. If I spend more time with Jill than with Him, again, we get out of balance.

God created us and provided the bible as the instruction manual to teach us how to live most effectively. In it, he reveals how to be a good spouse, parent and leader. Without developing our relationship with Him, how can we expect to understand how to be the best spouse, parent or leader we can be?

If you had a question about your washing machine, would you rather talk to the person who designed it, or the person at the store who sold it to you?

My mom taught me that life is about relationships. God taught me that life *is* all about relationships; the *right ones*, in the *right priority*.

Are you spending your time with the right relationships, in the right priority?

- What are your right relationships?
- What is the right priority?

Lets explore your top relationships and see if we can uncover opportunities for increased peace, joy and happiness.

Your Relationship With God

> *Love the Lord your God with all your heart and with all your soul and with all your mind. This is the first and greatest commandment.*

—Matthew 22:37–38

How would you describe your relationship with God? Are you like best friends who share everything? Are you more like acquaintances? Or are you wondering what exactly is required to have a relationship with God?

No matter where you are today, God is interested in developing and growing a personal relationship with you. No matter who you are, and no matter where you've come from.

If we decided to call the President of the United States today, could we do it? Even if we had the phone number for the White House you might agree that it would be difficult to get him on the phone. He's probably very busy, talking to important people, making important decisions. Even if we could miraculously get him on the phone, how much time do you think he would spend with us? Probably not much.

How much bigger is God, than the President? After all, He *is* the creator of the universe. His decisions focus on things like when the sun will rise or how to design six billion unique people on earth.

Believe it or not, God is waiting for your call. Not only is He waiting for your call, He can't wait to talk to you. He's interested to hear how you're doing. He's interested in what you're thinking and feeling. He's interested in spending time with you. He's interested in developing a relationship with you. He's got so much to tell you, show you, and teach you.

The interesting thing is that you can get God, the creator of the universe, almost immediately. You have his cell number and his e-mail address. The phone is never busy and the server is never down. You have direct access, and he's always available to talk.

You develop and grow your relationship with God, just as you would anyone else. It takes time, effort, and a desire to know the person. You wouldn't expect to know everything about your spouse within the first week after you met. The same is true with God, knowing Him takes time.

You wouldn't sit on the couch, click the remote night after night, and expect your marriage to get stronger, would you? You might actually have to turn off the TV, talk, listen, and make an effort to understand your spouse. The same is true with God; it takes some effort on your part.

Do you want to be a better spouse? Build your relationship with God and he'll show you what to do. Do you want to be a better parent? Build your relationship with God, and he'll show you how to do it. Do you want to be a better leader, employee, or friend? Build your relationship with God and he'll reveal the wisdom you need. It all starts with God.

> *Look to the Lord and his strength,*
> *Seek his face always.*

> —Psalm 105:4

Your relationship with your spouse

When God designed the marriage relationship, he created a special gift for you and me. Not many things on earth compare to the rewards we receive from living according to His plan for marriage. When you see a rock solid marriage, you usually find several things at the center of it. First, the foundation is God. Second, you see love, according to God's definition:

Love is patient,
love is kind.

It does not envy,
it does not boast,
it is not proud

It is not self-seeking,
it is not easily angered.
It keeps no records of wrongs.

Love does not rejoice in evil,
but rejoices with truth.

It always protects, always trusts,
always hopes, always perseveres.
Love never fails....

—1 Corinthians 13:4–8

Think back to when you first met your spouse. Do you remember long conversations and time evaporating? Did love make you do some pretty unusual things?

When Jill and I first met, we did everything together. We went out for ice cream, played softball, and ran races. We went out to dinner, movies and concerts. My world instantly got brighter.

I remember my routine to get ready for our dates. Wash the car, inside and out. Select the perfect music. Spend more time than necessary getting ready, and double check the plans. Every detail was planned out. Although it never seemed like it, there was a lot of effort that went into preparing to see her. But it was a labor of love.

Have you seen the movie, *The Notebook*, with James Garner? If you want to see the power of love between a husband and wife, watch this movie. As Noah (James

Garner) is reflecting on his life, he says something that I thought was pretty cool:

"I'm just a common man with common thoughts. I've led a common life. There are no monuments dedicated to me, and my name will soon be forgotten. But I've loved another with all my heat and soul, and this will always be enough."

When I reflect on the best memories from my life, I think of Jill. The movie reminded me of all the experiences we've shared; the times we've laughed and cried together, and the thousands of interesting conversations we've shared. It reminded me of the struggles we've overcome and what we have to look forward to. It reminded me of the greatest gift God gave me, besides eternal life. The gift of my beautiful, loving wife, Jill.

God gives us many tools to build our relationships. As you grow into the lighthouse God intended for your spouse, lean on God's wisdom:

> *Be quick to listen, slow to speak, and slow to become angry.*
>
> —James 1:19

> *Do not let the sun go down while you are still angry.*
>
> —Ephesians 4:26

Your relationship with your children

Growing up as a kid, Dad was the center of my universe. All I wanted to do is spend time with him. If he was getting gas for the car, then I wanted to go. If he was raking leaves, then I wanted to also. Dad gave me the most valuable thing he could have given me; his time.

Your children are the same way. If they're at the age that you're still cool, then they want to spend time with you. If your children are still small, they want to be with you, even if its something exciting, like taking out the trash or returning a movie rental. You may not think it's a big deal, but they do. Never underestimate the power of spending time with your kids.

Never underestimate the power of spending time with your kids

Ask yourself if you've been the lighthouse God intended for your children. Are you training them up in the way they should go?

> *Train a child in the way he should go, and when he is old he will not turn from it.*

—Proverbs 22:6

Lets say you're on the computer, and your child comes in and asks you a question. You respond by saying, "In a minute honey, Mommy's busy." What the child sees is that the computer is more important than them. If you would just stop and take care of their little request, you'll notice they might not want you to rebuild their bike. They might just need a hug. Thirty seconds later they will be on their way.

How much time have you spent over the last week, one-on-one, with your children? The national average is about 7 minutes per day.

Sometimes we rationalize and say things like, "when this happens, or that happens, then I'll spend more time with the kids." Pretty soon the kids are all grown up and you spent your whole life preparing and forgot to do some "living."

In order to build a rock solid foundation with your kids, you must spend time with them. The more time you spend with them, the stronger your foundation will be. Lean on God's wisdom for building your relationship with your kids:

> *Be quick to listen, slow to speak, and slow to become angry.*
>
> —James 1:19

> *Let us not become weary in doing good, for at the proper time we will reap a harvest if we do not give up.*
>
> —Galatians 6:9

Looking at Your Relationships as a Leader

Thinking about what you do for a living, and the organization in which you work, who are the most important relationships in your work life? Think in terms of you being successful. Who must you build relationships with in order to be the best leader possible?

		Example:
1.	_____	1. Jeff (Boss)
2.	_____	2. Trisha (Assistant)
3.	_____	3. Brooke
4.	_____	4. Mitchell
5.	_____	5. Sandy

If you're a sales manager, you might build relationships with the service manager, or operations manager in order to lead and guide your people more effectively.

Questions

1. Are there any relationships you are overlooking, that if built, might add to your success as a leader?

2. What are your "right" work relationships, and what is the "right" priority?

3. Is it possible to double your effectiveness as a leader by doubling the depth, quality and strength of your most important work relationships?

4.　　What are three creative, fun and painless ways you can build your relationships with these people?

The Key to Successful Organizations

Every successful business is built on rock solid relationships.

Your business will only be as successful as your relationships are solid. If you want to grow your business, then grow your relationships.

The right relationships, in the right priority for each business will be different. The foundation of any good business is its people. These relationships are often overlooked and underestimated. While struggling businesses focus on building external relationships, successful businesses focus on building internal relationships.

In the average law firm, eighty percent of the clients come from only twenty percent of the employees; the partners. Because they understand the value of cultivating good relationships, they are involved in community service, serve on boards, and accept leadership roles outside of the daily law practice. They understand their business is only as good as the foundation, or their relationships.

Growing Your Foundation of Relationships is Key

I did business with a guy in Indianapolis. In the summers we would go to lunch and sit outside to enjoy the sunny day while talking business. During our conversations, he would look at everything and anything but me. A woman would walk by and his eyes were like a magnet. He would scan the restaurant for people he knew, and frequently would tell me to "hold on" while he got up to say hello. He would answer his cell phone in the middle of our conversations. He was Mr. Important.

He was there but he wasn't *there*. He was never "present" during our conversations. The result is that I never really felt important to him and lost interest in doing business with him. He missed several opportunities for new clients over the next few years.

When you spend time with God, your spouse, and your children, do you think of other things? I've caught myself thinking about work while playing with the kids. I've caught myself thinking about other things when Jill was talking. My mind has drifted when reading the Bible or praying.

What does this do to our relationships? Do you think God, your spouse and your kids know when you're not "there"? You bet they do, and it makes them feel unimportant.

Do you plan time to spend with God, your spouse, and your kids? Or do you just try to fit it in around work, and all the other "important" things you've got going on? Have you ever said you would spend time with them and then broke your promise? Was your excuse a phone call or staying late at work?

A key ingredient to growing any relationship is time. The formula for growing any relationship is:

- Plan time
- Spend time
- Be present

If you want to grow your relationship with God, you first must plan it. If you want to grow your marriage, plan time to spend alone. If you want to know your children more, plan the time to spend with them. You must plan the time, spend the time, and be "present" in the moment with them. The important thing to remember is not where you are, but where you're growing.

> ***The important thing to remember is not where you are, but where you're growing.***

Try an experiment. See if you experience more peace, joy and happiness in proportion to the amount of time and effort you spend building your relationships with God, your spouse, and your children.

Summary

Lighthouses must be built on rock solid foundations. A fulfilling life is built on rock solid relationships; the right ones in the right priority. Choose to build a strong foundation at home and at work by focusing on your "right" relationships in the right priority. Plan time, spend time, and be present in your conversations and watch your relationships blossom. Remember, your success at home or at work is dependant on the strength of your relationships; the right ones, in the right priority.

Your Right Relationships, in the Right Priority

Personal   Work

1.   1.

2.   2.

3.   3.

4.   4.

5.   5.

**Take-Away Formula
for Growing Relationships**

- **Plan time**

- **Spend time**

- **Be present**

UNIQUE
CHARACTER

ROCK SOLID FOUNDATION

Chapter 3
Understanding Your Unique Character

Each lighthouse is known by its size, shape and color. It's known by the distinct pattern of flashes, the radio signal, and the foghorn. When a sea captain is trying to identify a lighthouse, he refers to *The Book of Lights*. It describes the unique character of each of the 50,000 lighthouses.

Rainman

I had the privilege of playing baseball in college. We had guys on the team from many different states. Each year, because of the spring weather in Indiana, we traveled to Florida to play the first ten games of the season.

During one trip we discovered something unusual about one of our teammates. Driving back to the hotel after a game, we were trying to figure out our batting averages for the trip. One guy said, " I got 16 hits in 33 at bats." We were looking for a calculator when our quiet second baseman, Paul, murmured in a soft voice, "That's about .480" Everybody laughed and kept looking for the calculator.

Then somebody else said, "I'm 9 for 24, what's that?" "Oh, that's about .380." said Paul. We looked at him like he might be serious and then found the calculator. Somebody ran the numbers, and sure enough he was right. We all looked at him like he was a freak, then someone from the back of the bus yelled, "Rainman!" For the rest of the season nobody bothered looking for the calculator, we just asked Paul.

You're A One-Of-A-Kind

Just like Paul, you have many distinct characteristics. Your fingerprints and voice pattern. The words you choose to describe different things. You like certain movies, music, and restaurants. Certain things make you laugh that other people don't "get". You excel at things that others struggle with.

Take a look at your thumb. Notice the pattern of your thumbprint. Look at it closely and notice the swirling pattern of the lines. If there are six billion people on the planet today, and everybody's thumbprint is different, how could that possibly be? I can think of a few patterns, but do some people have a checkerboard, and others have lightning bolts? It is truly amazing to think that we are all totally unique.

The important thing is to celebrate who you are and be grateful you're not somebody else. You are a one-of-a-kind, limited edition, custom built home. God gave you special gifts:

> *God has given gifts to each of you from his great variety of spiritual gifts. Manage them well so that God's generosity can flow through you. Are you called to be a speaker? Then speak as though God himself were speaking*

through you. Are you called to help others? Do it with all the strength and energy that God supplies. Then God will be given glory in everything through Jesus Christ. All glory and power belong to him forever and ever. Amen.

—1 Peter 4:10–11

Just be Yourself

I can remember growing up always trying to be somebody else. Playing baseball as a kid, we always tried to swing like our favorite professional players. We soon realized that a perfect swing for one guy was not good for the next. Our bodies are made differently, so what's good for you will probably not be good for me.

Are you trying to be somebody else? Do you get discouraged when you see a neighbor or family member succeeding in some area of their life that you're struggling in? What normally happens is we compare the strength of another person with a weakness of ourselves. That is the formula for discouragement.

Think about it. Who is the most successful person you know? What are they good at? Now think of your three greatest strengths. Can you do anything better than they can? When you compare your strengths to their weaknesses, you fair much better. So the next time you begin feeling inferior, check to make sure you're not comparing their strengths to your weaknesses. And just remember, you'll be happiest when you just be yourself.

Play To Your Strengths

Imagine if the lighthouse compared itself to the sun? It would sound something like this, "I'm not as good as the sun. The sun can light up half of the planet at once. I can only reach 35 miles out." Or what if your night-light got upset because it only has power to light a bedroom and not a dark night? Now imagine if you had a lighthouse in your bedroom instead of your night-light. My guess is that your retinas would burn out from the bright light if the foghorn didn't give you a heart attack first.

Does your job allow you to fully use your strengths? I have an interesting experience from early in my career.

For about a decade, I was in a career that didn't play to my strengths. After a couple years working for a company, I would get the urge to look around and see what other "bigger and better" jobs were out there. I was either bored or not being challenged, so I made several job changes. The result was climbing to the top of the corporate ladder only to realize that the ladder was leaning against the wrong tree.

My college friend Andy, graduated and began a job he enjoyed and was very good at. He loved what he did and wasn't concerned with what others thought.

The only time I would see him was his yearly trip to Indianapolis, for the Indy 500. Our tradition was to pack the little white truck full of supplies, and head down to the middle of the track. We would set up our lawn chairs, catch up, laugh, and enjoy the sun. We did this eight years in a row.

Our conversations consisted of me trying to convince him of how "well" I was doing, while he would share what he was learning. Each year he seemed to grow happier and more fulfilled, while I became more dissatisfied with my career.

Looking back I realize that Andy was playing to his strengths and I was fooling myself. Andy was far more successful, because he knew what he was good at, and played to his strengths. How about you? What are your strengths?

Things I love to do:

1.
2.
3.
4.
5.

Things I'm good at:

1.
2.
3.
4.
5.

Things others say I'm good at:

1.
2.
3.
4.
5.

Things I do for fun:

1.
2.
3.
4.
5.

Things people like about me:

1.
2.
3.
4.
5.

Things I've been trained in

1.
2.
3.
4.
5.

Things I love in my current job: Hobbies I love:

1.   1.

2.   2.

3.   3.

4.   4.

5.   5.

Every Person You Lead Has a Unique Character

Have you heard the story about Acres of Diamonds? Russell Conwell tells of a story that was told to him in 1870, on a trip down the Tigris River.

A farmer heard about vast diamond mines in far away lands. The more he learned about them, the more he wanted one for his own. He began dreaming of what he could do with the beautiful stones, and what it would provide for his family.

He went to a wise man and asked where he could find them. In order to pay for his journey, he sold his farm, and had his family stay with neighbors until he returned.

After years of wandering all over Europe looking for diamonds, the farmer died without finding a single stone.

Shortly after he died, his successor who purchased his old farm was down at the stream that ran through the farm. He discovered a shiny stone that was attached to a black rock. He took it into his house, set it on the table and forgot about it.

A few days later the wise man came to visit and noticed the shiny stone on the table. He said, "What a beautiful diamond!" The farmer was puzzled and said that it was just a stone he found in his stream. Together they went out back and began digging in the stream and discovered one of the largest diamond mines the world has ever seen.

If the farmer had just taken the time to understand what he already had, he would have saved himself years of trouble. If he could have only recognized what was right under his nose, it would have prevented heartache, stress, and tears. It would have provided him everything he was searching for.

Have you discovered the acres of diamonds under your nose? Do you understand the unique character of each and every person you are leading? Let's see if you do:

1. Can you name which of the five main storms of life (*Job, Money, Marriage, Health, Family*) your top five work relationships are dealing with? Which is their strongest?

2. If every job paid a million dollars per year, what would they do? What did they dream of becoming when they were younger?

3. Have you ever spent time with them, during your personal time? Ever had them over to your house for dinner?

Many leaders are constantly searching for the "right" people when they have everything they need right under their noses.

Before you go searching for the "perfect" employee, take the time and effort to fully understand the unique character of each person you have been given the privilege to lead. You might be pleasantly surprised at what you can find.

I was in St. Louis leading a team building retreat for the executives of an upscale furniture store. In order to get their brains moving, we did an icebreaker to start the day.

We had them pair up and ask each other three questions. They first thought it was silly, because nearly everyone had worked together for over two decades. They had seen each other's children grow up, so they thought they really knew each other. As we went around the room and the laughter erupted, the most common response was, "I didn't know that about you".

Lighthouse leaders know their people more than average leaders. Lighthouse leaders understand what makes each of their individual people "tick". Lighthouse leaders care enough about their people to spend the time and effort to understand their unique character.

Many people ask for the most important things to know about the people they are leading. Following is a list of ten things you should know about every person you are attempting to lead:

1. What do they do for fun? What are they passionate about? Why?

2. Which of the five main storms of life are they dealing with now? How long have they been dealing with it?

3. How would they describe *their* perfect leader? Why?

4.   What is their description of their perfect work-
        ing environment? Why?

5.   What did they always dream of becoming? Why?

6.   What are the five things you have in common
        with them? What is the single belief, experience,
        or thing you have most in common?

7.   What are they really good at and what do they
        dread doing? Why?

8.   Know their personality profile (DISC) or other
        assessment.

9.   What motivates them? Why?

10.   Do they love working for you? If not, what
        would make them love working for you? Why?

As you spend time with your people and get to know
them, you will have opportunities to ask these questions.
If you just sit them down for 15 minutes and expect
them to open up and give you these answers, you'll get
the answer they think you're looking for.

You'll find out your most valuable information when you
ask the "why" on the end of each question. Try it and see
for yourself. Remember the key to great conversations is
to let the other person talk. Make it a goal to learn one
more thing about each person when you spend an
extended amount of time with them.

Are you getting their best ideas?

Research shows that employees in corporate America hold
back 80% of their best ideas. The reason might have

something to do with their environment. Employees need to feel safe, appreciated, respected, and loved. They need to know that you have their best interest at heart. The stress level must be low. They need to be doing things they love and are good at, not things they aren't good at. It is similar to how a greenhouse works.

Lets say you wanted to grow tropical plants but live in a cold climate. You build a greenhouse and buy the seeds. What do you do next? You would probably learn everything you could about creating the best environment for your plants. You would find out what temperature and how much moisture was needed. You would probably think of ways you could help them grow, and even flourish under your care.

Just like every plant, every person needs the right conditions to grow and develop into their full potential. You as a leader must do everything in your control make sure your "greenhouse" is set up for maximum growth and development. If they aren't growing and thriving under your care, the first place to check is your "greenhouse".

Every Business has a Unique Character

Every business has a unique character. Its individual employees, customers, suppliers, managers, vendors, service providers, product, price, placement and method of promotion. Its phone numbers and web addresses. Its location and starting date.

Even though there may be thousands of organizations that appear to be just like yours, you are all truly unique.

Understand your unique character and you will understand how to best to position yourselves in the marketplace. Understand your unique relationships, and you will find advantages. Understand your unique people and you will find advantages. Understand your unique customers and you will find even more advantages. The more you understand your unique character, the more effective an organization you will be.

Summary

Just as none of the 50,000 lighthouses are exactly alike, none of the six billion humans are alike. You're a one-of-a-kind, custom built home. Every employee has a unique character. Create a "greenhouse" for growth. Stop trying to be somebody else and just be yourself. Start playing to your strengths and shine your own unique light. When you do this you will experience more fulfillment in your life as a leader and as a person.

KNOWS
ITS
PURPOSE

UNIQUE
CHARACTER

ROCK SOLID FOUNDATION

Chapter 4
Knowing Your Purpose

The Architect Had a Purpose

Before each lighthouse was designed and built, the architect had to understand the specific purpose of the structure. He had to take many factors into consideration to determine the best size, shape and building materials to use. He needed to understand the elements it would face; average wind speed, force of the waves, and potential for hurricanes. Only when the purpose was crystal clear to the architect did he begin designing it.

Just as the lighthouse was designed and built for a purpose, so were you.

God Had a Purpose

> *For we are God's workmanship, created in Christ Jesus to do good works, which God prepared in advance for us to do.*
>
> —Ephesians 2:10

The lighthouse helps the most people when it does what it was made to do. You will help the most people, be the most fulfilled, and experience the most success, when you discover your God given purpose, and begin living it.

Did you know that God created you for a specific purpose? Just like a recipe for cookies, he mixed specific ingredients, in specific amounts to create you. A cup of creativity, a teaspoon of passion and a dash of humor. There is nobody else on the planet that has the exact combination of ingredients, in the same amounts, that you have.

According to Rick Warren, Author of *The Purpose Driven Life*, God created us for five main purposes:

1. For God's Pleasure
2. For God's Family
3. To Become like Christ
4. To Serve God
5. A Specific Mission

We are going to focus on your specific mission in this book.

Federal Express Knows Its Purpose

What is Fed Ex known for? They focus on overnight delivery. They don't try and be all things to all people. They don't try and compete with the U.S. mail or local courier services. They do what they do best, and forget the rest. They grow rich in a niche. The most successful businesses know their purpose, shine their light, and attract clients.

Discover Your Purpose

Did you ever see Michael Jordan play basketball? He was born to play the game. He seemed to move effortlessly up and down the court, and always seemed to "see" what was going to happen before anybody else. He was always **two** steps ahead. Millions of people around the world tuned in to see him do his thing. He was born to play basketball.

When you discover your purpose, you will move through your day effortlessly, and flow from one task to the other. Time will go so fast. You will be happier, more fulfilled and feel like you're making a contribution.

Do you remember when he Michael Jordan decided to play baseball? He wasn't as smooth on the diamond as he was on the court. He didn't have as much success playing baseball as he did playing basketball. His purpose was to play basketball, and that is where he had most of his success. You too, will have most of your success when you discover and live your purpose.

Ways to Discover Your Purpose
Ask God

If God created you with a specific task in mind, would it make sense to ask Him what you were created for? Would it make sense to seek his guidance through reading the Bible? Would it make sense to knock on his door? Just like the washing machine example, the best place for answers is the person who designed you.

> ***Ask*** *and it will be given to you;* ***seek*** *and you will find;* ***knock*** *and the door will be opened to you. For everyone who asks receives; he who seeks finds; and to him who knocks, the door will be opened.*

—Matthew 7:7–8

Seven Ways God Speaks To You

Bill, the pastor at our church, and I were having lunch at a local Mexican restaurant. I asked him how God speaks to us. He said that God speaks to us in seven main ways:

- His Word
- Prayer
- Peace of God
- Wise Counsel
- Circumstances
- Timing
- Divine signs or instruction

His Word

We speak to God through prayer, and God speaks to us through His Word, or the Bible. Bill's advice is to read your Bible daily. He recommends consistent, daily reading, even if it's a few minutes per day. He has read his entire bible over thirty times, and does this by spending a few minutes each day.

Prayer

Bill said prayer consists of talking and *listening*. He said the more we pray, the more we will grow in our ability to recognize God's voice. Bill said spending time with God is the only way to grow our relationship with Him. Some people spend a few minutes each day praying, while others spend a couple hours. Some pray in the car and others pray in a quiet spot at home. Pour your heart out to God and see what happens.

Peace of God

God gives us peace that rules our heart and emotions, when He is guiding and directing us. If you have two choices to make and have peace with one, and no peace with the other, that is an indication as to which way God is leading.

For example, if you are wondering if you should buy a car or keep the one you have, you can ask God for direction. After you ask God in prayer, pay attention to what you feel about each choice. You might have peace with one choice and something might not feel right about the other.

Or you might be hiring for a position and have narrowed it down to two people, who both look great on paper. They both interview well, your staff liked them, and their references check out equally well. You might want to ask God for the wisdom to select the best candidate. You pray about them, and after several days you feel a peace about one more than the other.

Wise Counsel

Seek wise people for advice to understand what God might be telling you. Bill said that wise counsel always sends you back into the hands of God. You ask them a question and they think of scripture that applies, or have you pray about something specific.

For example, you have an employee who is not performing well. You do everything in your power to help them get back on track and still no improvement. You can't figure out what to do, so you call three people who have a relationship with God and have probably dealt with similar situations. They agree to meet and ask you questions to understand the situation.

Truly wise council listens more than they talk. They seek to understand your situation and then figure out which biblical principles apply. They might be reminded of a scripture. They might be reminded of a story from the bible, where a person handled a similar situation. Wise council limits their personal opinion and seeks to put you back into the hands of God. They know that you and God make your decisions.

Circumstances

During your daily life, you might hear a song on the radio or somebody might give you a bible verse. You might see a billboard or a bumper sticker. You might get a timely call.

For example, you might be wondering if you should hire another person for your department. The budget is available, and your people are asking for more help. You know that you can go another six months before you absolutely need someone. You pray about it and a week later you get two calls from friends who refer people to you who would be perfect for your department.

Timing

The timing of when things come to you. You might be praying about moving to Florida or Arizona, and want God to help you make that decision. Several days later you might receive an e-mail with a reference to Arizona. Then you watch a movie that night and it takes place in Arizona. You might get a call from a friend you haven't spoken to in years, who just moved to Arizona. The timing of it all is the key.

Divine Signs or Instruction

Bill said God speaks to us though our dreams or visions. You might wake up with the answer to a problem. You might have a dream about finding an important file in an unexpected place in your office.

How You Know When God is Speaking

> *But the wisdom that comes from heaven is first of all pure; then peace-loving, considerate, submissive, full of mercy and good fruit, impartial and sincere.*

> —James 3:17

Bill also says God will confirm His answers by speaking to us in several ways. For example, you read something in the bible, then you hear a song on the radio that says the same thing. You might start thinking about it in prayer, and then see a bible verse at church that says the same thing. Or God might flood you with one bible verse from many different sources. The more frequent and varied ways it comes to you, the greater the chances are that God is speaking to you.

Seek Answers

Take a day off and go to a park with a notebook. Plan to do nothing but think. Write down what you would do if you received a check for $1 million dollars, and could pay your living expenses in full, for the next five years. The only requirement was that you had to figure out a way to serve other people.

If this sounds silly, think of Siskel and Ebert. They were probably sitting around watching movies and their conversation probably went like this, " Man, if we could get paid to do this, I would be in heaven." At that moment they probably looked at each other while their eyes got real big. My guess is they got out a notebook and started figuring out how they would do it.

What do you love to do? What are you good at? Take a look at the following questions and see if that reveals any clues:

- What are your five greatest assets?

- What three things do you do better than most people?
- What do you think about during the day?
- Who has a job, occupation or work situation that appears to be perfect for you?
- What kinds of things do people compliment you on at work or at home?

Live Your Purpose

You might know your purpose but fear might be standing in the way of you living it. For example, you know that God made you to be a teacher, and to change careers seems impossible. You might need additional education that takes time and money. Lean on God's wisdom:

Look to the Lord and his strength; seek his face always.

—Psalm 105:4

With man this is impossible, but not with God; all things are possible with God.

—Mark 10:27

Ask God if the timing is right

Just like the disciple Peter during the storm, when he wanted to walk on the water. The other disciples in the boat probably wanted to do the same, but fear paralyzed them. Peter took a risk but asked Jesus if he should come. What happened next? Jesus told him to come out of the boat and trust Him. It was only then that Peter stepped out of the boat, onto the crashing waves and walked on water.

The waves didn't calm down *before* he stepped out. He had to make the first move, and so it is with you. You must ask God if He wants you to do this. By doing this you can rely on His strength and ability and not yours. Many of you are relived to hear this, as I was.

You might have to take some action before God steps in to help you. If you're expecting it to happen overnight, you might be disappointed. If you're expecting it to be really easy, you might be fooling yourself. If you're afraid to fail, then stay in the boat. But if you want to experience the power and exhilaration of God working through you, then step out of the boat.

If you want to read a great book about discovering and living your purpose, read *If You Want to Walk On Water, You Gotta Get Out Of The Boat,* by John Ortman.

> *Nothing matters more than knowing God's purposes for your life, and nothing can compensate for not knowing them.*

—Rick Warren

Your Purpose as a Lighthouse Leader

You might be a leader at work or at home. You might be a leader in your neighborhood, alumni association, your circle of friends or your sports team. Wherever God has placed you in a position of authority, he has done so with a specific purpose.

What is God's purpose for you as a leader? Think of the people you lead and think of what you can do for them. Do some people need encouragement and praise? Do some need to be corrected and instructed? Do some need a person to listen to them and make them feel important? Others might need your insight into experiences you've had or specific knowledge you have.

Regardless of the arena you are leading, your main purpose is to grow your people. Managers enforce rules and procedures. Lighthouse leaders grow people. Lighthouse leaders know that the formula for growing their organization is growing their people.

If your purpose is to grow your people, your job is to figure out which direction to grow them. Ask them where they want to grow. Ask yourself which area they need to grow and develop. Compare the two and develop a plan.

Have you noticed that small children are happy most of the time? Why is that? One of the main reasons is that they are learning something new almost every week. They are constantly learning how to do or say something new. They are constantly growing.

Your people are the same way. If they aren't growing, they're dying. If you aren't consciously growing them, and they aren't growing themselves, they are slowly dying on the inside. If they're dying on the inside, you need to ask yourself what you're doing or not doing as their leader. You need to ask yourself if you're being the Lighthouse leader God intended them to follow.

Summary

Just as each lighthouse was built for a purpose, so were you. God gave you a purpose before you were born. Spend time with Him to understand what you were made for. Remember to:

- Ask
- Seek
- Knock

It all starts with God. Once you discover your purpose ask God for the courage to live it. Nothing in your vocation will be more fulfilling than when you start living your purpose. If you're wondering what exactly God has in store for you, keep seeking His face until he reveals it:

> *"For I know the plans I have for you,"*
> *declares the Lord, " plans to prosper you and*
> *not to harm you, plans to give you hope and a*
> *future. Then you will call upon me and come*
> *and pray to me, and I will listen to you. You*
> *will seek me and find me when you seek me*

with all your heart. I will be found by you,"
declares the Lord…

—Jeremiah 29:11

Figure out your purpose as a leader. Understand that
growing people is one of the most rewarding experiences
you'll have in life. Understand which direction to grow
them and make a plan.

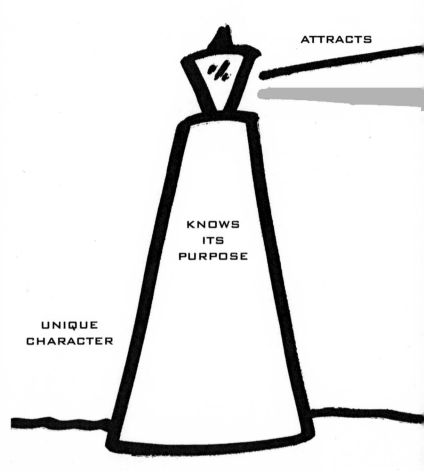

ATTRACTS

KNOWS
ITS
PURPOSE

UNIQUE
CHARACTER

ROCK SOLID FOUNDATION

Chapter 5
Attracting People To You

Just as a lighthouse, you attract people in proportion to your "attractiveness". For the lighthouse, it means removing the "dirt" off the glass. It means a fully functioning bulb. It means properly positioned lenses and mirrors. But none of this matters unless it is build on a rock solid foundation, understands its unique character, and knows it purpose.

The same is true for you. If your foundation of relationships is faulty, if you're trying to be somebody you're not, and don't know your purpose, you'll have to work extra hard to have an attractive personality. In this chapter we'll discuss how to polish your personality for maximum attractiveness.

The Power of Positive Attraction

Who is the most positive person you know? For me, it's my sister-in-law Trisha. She always has something positive to say. She always brings light to a situation. She's fun to be around. She is always encouraging.

People want to be around positive people. They're like people-magnets. Take Jesus for example. He is the ultimate people magnet:

> *Jesus left there and went along to the Sea of Galilee. Then he went up on the mountainside and sat down. Great **crowds came to him**, bringing the lame, the blind, the crippled, the mute and laid them at his feet.*

—Matthew 15:29–30

Jesus is the master at attracting people. Why is this? What kind of personality traits did he possess when he walked the earth? Lets look to see if scripture can reveal anything. According to Galatians 5:22–23, it says that the fruit of the Spirit is:

- Love
- Joy
- Peace
- Patience
- Kindness
- Goodness
- Faithfulness
- Gentleness
- Self-Control

Jesus was attractive because he was humble. He listened. He focused on the other person. He spoke the truth. As you study the bible, and the way he treated people, you see something brilliant. Not only did he shine his light and emit the fruit of the Spirit, but he did four things that attracted people like bugs to a bug light.

People responded. They couldn't get enough of his teaching, his comfort and his wisdom. They walked miles just to be in his presence. He attracted children and adults. He attracted the sick and the healthy. Jesus was and did the following:

- Available for people
- Present for people
- Served people
- Forgave people

Available For People

Jesus was the most compassionate person who walked the earth. He would drop everything to help others. He was quick to help and slow to judge. He was attractive because he was available.

- When Jesus was told that the ruler's daughter had just died and was asked to come and heal her, he got up and went. (Matthew 9:18–19)

- When the centurion came up to Jesus and asked for help to heal his servant that was paralyzed and suffering, Jesus said, "*I will go and heal him*." (Matthew 8:5–7)

- When Jesus wanted to go rest and five thousand people followed him and gathered around, he had compassion on them and began teaching them many things. (Mark 6:32–34)

When your spouse, children or employees want to spend time with you, are you available like Jesus was? Would they agree with your answer? If not, don't worry. You can start today and watch your "attractiveness" grow.

Present for People

Another reason Jesus had such an attractive personality, was because he was present for people. Even if they needed his attention for just a few minutes, He would *stop and focus* on them.

- Jesus was approaching Jericho and a blind beggar called out to him. Jesus stopped and asked, "What do you want me to do for you?" The man said, "Lord, I want to see". Immediately Jesus restored his sight, and he was on his way. (Luke 18:35–43).

When people need your attention, do you stop and focus like Jesus did? Your spouse, children and employees need you to be present. If you haven't been as "present" as you should, that's not unusual. Don't beat yourself up, just begin today and watch your "attractiveness quotient" multiply.

- Jesus was walking down the mountainside while large crowds of people were following him. A man with leprosy came before him and said, "Lord, if you are willing, you can make me clean." Jesus reached out his hand and touched the man and said, "I am wiling...be clean!". Immediately he was cured. (Matthew 8:1–3)

Being present for people requires you to *stop and focus* on them. Many times you can meet their needs immediately.

Served them

The greatest among you will be your servant.
Whoever exalts himself will be humbled, and
whoever humbles himself will be exalted.

—Mathew 23:12

Jesus didn't walk around bragging about who he was, who his dad was, and what he had accomplished. He made it very clear by his actions, that he wants us to serve people. One byproduct of serving people is an attractive personality.

Greater love has no one than this, that he lay
down his life for his friends.

—John 15:13

It's interesting that when large crowds gathered around Jesus, he didn't start signing autographs and soak up the attention. He was concerned about their needs. He served them.

- When Jesus landed and saw the large crowd, he had compassion on them and healed their sick. (Matthew 14:14)
- When the disciples wanted to send the 5,000 people away because it was getting late, Jesus had them stay and fed them until they were satisfied. (Matthew 14:15–20)

One of the reasons Jesus had an attractive personality was because he had a heart to serve. The more he served people, the more they were attracted to him. The same is true with you. The more you serve the people in your life, the more they will be attracted to you.

Forgave them

Be gentle and ready to forgive; never hold grudges. Remember, the Lord forgave you, so you must forgive others.

—Colossians 3:13

Peter came to Jesus and asked how many times should he forgive someone who does him wrong. Peter guessed and said, "Up to seven times?" Jesus answered, *I tell you, not seven times, but **seventy seven** times."* (Matthew 18:21–22)

Has anybody done you wrong? Do you know anybody that you could forgive today, that might be lugging the weight of guilt around, as a result of hurting you? It feels good for everybody when we forgive.

It's interesting when we look at the parable of the unmerciful servant. When the servant owed the king more than he could pay back, the king ordered his entire family to be sold to repay the debt. When the servant fell on his knees and begged for mercy, the king took pity on him, cancelled his debt, and let him go.

But when the same servant went out and found a fellow servant who owed him money he refused to forgive him, and had him put in prison until he could pay the debt.

When the king got wind of this, he called the first servant back in and was pretty mad. He said, "I cancelled that debt of yours because you begged me to. Shouldn't you have mercy on your fellow servant just as I had on you?" In his anger the king turned him over to the jailers until he paid back all he owed. (Matthew 18:21–35)

Have you ever been like the unmerciful servant? The more you forgive, the more attractive you will be.

The Greatest Gift of Forgiveness

Have you ever made any mistakes? Have you ever done anything you wish you hadn't? Ever wish you could wipe your slate clean?

Sometimes the weight of our mistakes or bad decisions takes away our peace. God didn't make us to be frustrated, upset and angry all the time. He didn't make us to be afraid, unsure and scared. He wants us to experience a life full of peace, purpose and meaning.

What happens is that because we're human, we make mistakes. We have minds of our own, and God gave us the ability to make our own decisions. Sometimes we choose to obey him, and sometimes we don't. When we disobey him, God calls that sin.

Now we don't have to kill someone, rob a bank, or have an affair to sin. We sin by losing our cool and yelling at our kids. We sin by telling a "white lie", or fudging on our taxes. We sin by not forgiving another person. How many people do you know that have never told a lie, never stolen anything, or never did anything wrong, their whole entire life? God says:

> *"For all have sinned and fall short of the glory of God."*

—Romans 3:23

All means *all*. That includes you and me, and everyone we know. As a result of our sin, we are separated from God.

What we try to do is make it up to God by being a "good person", by studying religion, or by trying to do good things, like giving money to the church. We think, "Well if I do these things, then God will appreciate these things, and maybe he'll let me into heaven." So ultimately we reason that if we do more good things than bad, then God will surely let us into heaven.

It doesn't work that way. God says that, *"There is a way that seems right to man, but in the end leads to death."*

—Proverbs 14:12

None of our efforts can bridge the gap we have created between ourselves and God. There is only one remedy for this problem of separation of God.

> *God is on one side and all the people on the other side, and Jesus Christ, Himself man, is between them to bring them together.*

—1 Timothy 2:5

> *Jesus said, "I am the way, the truth and the life. No man comes to the Father, except through me."*

—John 14:6

The Bible says that only way for you to get into heaven is to believe in Jesus Christ and receive Him as your savior.

> *"If you confess with your mouth "Jesus is Lord", and believe in your heart that God raised Him from the dead, you will be saved."*

—Romans 10:9

Wait a minute, you might be thinking. This sounds too easy or this doesn't make sense. What's the bottom line, what is required of me to get right with God and get into heaven?

1. *Admit your need (That you are a sinner)*

2. *Be willing to turn from your sins (Repent)*

3. *Believe that Jesus Christ died for you on the Cross and rose from the grave.*

4. *Through prayer, invite Jesus Christ to come in and control your life through the Holy Spirit. (Receive Him as Savior and Lord)*

(from Steps to Peace with God)

Is there any good reason you cannot receive Jesus Christ right now? If you want to, pray this prayer…

> Dear God,
>
> I know that I am a sinner and need Your forgiveness. I believe that Jesus Christ died for my sins. I am willing to turn from my sins. I now invite Jesus Christ to come into my heart and life as my personal Savior. I am willing, by God's strength, to follow and obey Jesus Christ as the Lord of my life.

If you prayed the prayer for the first time, you just made God smile. You are now one of God's children. He has been waiting for this moment your entire life. You have begun your relationship with God, so get ready to experience the abundant life. God is your heavenly Father and loves you more than you can imagine.

> *Everyone who calls on the name of the Lord will be saved.*

> —Romans 10:13

> *To all who received Him, to those who believed in His name, He gave the right to become the children of God.*

> —John 1:12

Understanding Your Attractiveness as a Leader

As you understand how Jesus led people, do you see ways to implement this into your leadership style? Can you benefit from his example of attracting people? The beauty of role models is that if we do the same things, we can get similar results.

As we look at the four components of the way Jesus attracted people, let's look at specific ways you can implement them into your workday.

Available

If you're available as a leader, you place a high priority on being there for your people. You drop things to listen to them. You place their needs above yours. If you were planning on having lunch by yourself and an employee really needed you, you would bring them along. You place people ahead of things. You make an effort to be attentive to their needs, and it is apparent to them. They know they have access to you. They have your cell phone and your home phone number and know that you are there for them.

Present

If you're a leader who is present for your people, you'll shut your office door to give them uninterrupted time with you. You won't take calls or check your e-mail during conversations. You listen to understand them more and to figure out how to help, as opposed to appease and get them out of your office.

If you're present as a leader you can recall details, information and things from past conversations. You either take notes and keep them in a file or you concentrate extra hard in order to remember key details, and you repeat them in future conversations. You focus on being the best listener in that person's life.

Serve

If you are a leader who serves, you open doors for them. You do something for them, that they can do for themselves, but do it anyway. You have an attitude that says, "I'm here to serve you." You think and believe that you are there for your people, rather than looking at them as tools to meet your goals.

If you serve your people, you might grab their lunch trash and throw it away. You might ask them if you can get them a cup of coffee or something to drink. You have an attitude of, "What can I get you? What can I do for you?"

Forgive

If you are a leader who forgives, you give them a clean slate after making mistakes. You give them room to fail and you are there to pick them up, not to pour salt in their wounds. A forgiving leader understands that making mistakes is part of the learning process and gives his people opportunities to grow from them.

A forgiving leader is not to be confused with being a doormat. If your employee is not truly sorry for the mistake, and doesn't show any remorse for doing wrong, then that is a different situation. There is a big difference between letting people walk all over you and having the ability to forgive mistakes.

In order to get a snapshot of your attractiveness quotient, let's take a small quiz:

Ask yourself these questions:

1. On a scale from 1–10 where do you rate as an attractive leader? A perfect 10 would be the Jesus example, and a 1 would be the worst leader you've ever followed.

2. How do you rate in the various components of attractiveness as a leader? Rate yourself for each component on a scale from 1–10:

    a. Available for them

    b. Present for them

    c. Serve them

    d. Forgive them

3.   Could you increase your attractiveness, as a
      leader if all you did was focus on these four
      components for the next 14 days?

This style may not feel right for you. This style might not
fit your personality or your people. The worst thing you
could do is to *assume* that it won't work and not try it.
The best-case scenario is that you try it, it works, and you
have a much better rapport with your people.

Summary

Just as a lighthouse, you attract people in proportion to
your "attractiveness". Jesus is the ultimate people magnet,
so we can learn how to attract from his example. He dis-
played the fruit of the Spirit:

- Love
- Joy
- Peace
- Patience
- Kindness
- Goodness
- Faithfulness
- Gentleness
- Self-Control

He also did certain things that caused people to want to
be around him. He was and did these things for people:

- Available
- Present
- Served
- Forgave

If you want to shine your light and achieve your maximum attractiveness to the people in your life, learn from the ultimate lighthouse, Jesus. When you model him, you'll be amazed at how many people will be drawn to you, and give you permission to guide them.

Take-Away Formula for Attracting People

- **Be available**
- **Be present**
- **Serve them**
- **Forgive them**

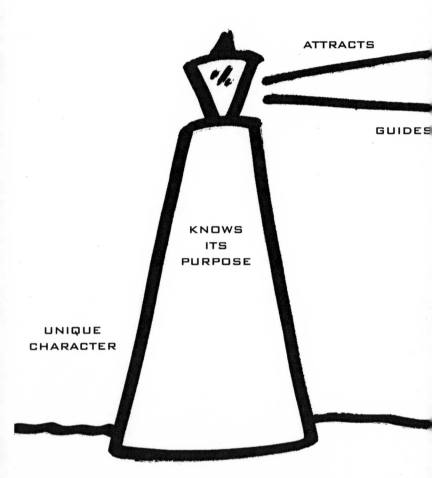

Chapter 6
Guiding People

Can the lighthouse guide ships to safety if the foundation crumbles and it is lying on its side? Would the lighthouse cause confusion if it produced flashes of light similar to other lighthouses along the coast? What would happen if a lighthouse decided to be a streetlight or light a Wal-Mart parking lot, instead of what it was made to do? Disaster. What if the lighthouse was dirty, and the light was dim? Ships might get too close to the rocks and crash. So guiding ships is dependant on all of these things coming together.

Let's recap the laws of the lighthouse:

- Rock Solid Foundation
- Unique Character
- Knows Its Purpose
- Attracts
- Guides

Permission to Guide

Think back to your school days. Who was your favorite teacher or professor? What was it about them that you liked? Did you work harder in their class than in others? Why is that?

One reason is you gave them permission to guide you. You put your trust in them, and you let them influence you. Do the people in your life give you permission to guide them?

Think of somebody in your life that rubs you the wrong way. What kind of influence do they have over your life? Probably little or none, unless they are in a position of authority over you.

Now lets see if we can learn from the ultimate lighthouse, Jesus.

1. Did he have a rock solid foundation with God the Father?

2. Did he have a unique character?

3. Did he know his purpose on earth?

4. Did he attract people?

5. Did he guide people?

> *The Lord says, "I will guide you along the*
> *best pathway for your life.*
> *I will advise you and watch over you.*

—Psalm 32:8

How did the "ultimate lighthouse" guide people?

The best example of how Jesus guided people is found in the training of the twelve disciples. Now, regardless of your faith, let's look at what he accomplished as a leader.

He passed a message on that is still being told two thousand years later. He chose twelve ordinary people to train in order to deliver the message and pass it on. He didn't choose the best public speakers, the most influential businessmen, or the most respected religious leaders. He chose twelve ordinary people, like you and me.

In order to pass on a message that would withstand the test of time, you might guess that he spent a decade or two training them. The amazing thing is that he only trained them for eighteen months. His ministry lasted three years, and the training of the disciples lasted eighteen short months. If you're wondering if Jesus' methods were effective, just look at the facts. Two thousand years after he taught twelve men, the lessons have been passed down to you and me.

To put this in perspective, ask yourself if what you've taught your employees or children will be passed down twelve generations.

When we look at the way Jesus prepared the disciples, we see the way he guided them breaks down into six fundamentals:

- He spent time with them
- He encouraged them
- He focused on training them
- He let them make mistakes
- He lovingly corrected and instructed them
- He prayed for them

He spent time with them

Basically they spent eighteen months with Jesus. They listened to his teachings, asked him questions, and saw how he dealt with the people. They traveled with him by boat and on foot. They saw him go away and pray very frequently (Matthew 14:23). They learned the most by watching him and witnessing how he did things in different situations.

If you're having difficulty influencing the people in your life, check to see if you're spending enough time with them. Many times you can dramatically improve your results just by spending more time with them.

He encouraged them

Jesus said positive things. He encouraged the disciples to try new things. He believed in them until they believed in themselves.

Do you encourage the people in your life? If not, don't worry. If it's not natural for you to encourage or say positive things to people, start small. Begin by saying three encouraging things per day to the people in your life.

He focused on training them

> *A student is not above his teacher, but everyone who is fully trained will be like his teacher.*

> —Luke 6:40

What Jesus is saying is that the people you are leading or guiding are not fully trained until they can perform at your level.

How many of your managers, professors, or parents trained you so well, that your level of competency reached theirs? Most leaders agree training is important, but few understand the level of training Jesus is suggesting. What would happen if you focused your energy and effort on training the people you lead, to the standard Jesus describes?

He let them make mistakes

Jesus knew how to teach people. First they traveled with him; watching, listening, and learning from his example. Next he sent them out on ministry opportunities and special assignments. This is where they would gain experience and apply what they learned. Jesus knew they would have challenges, make mistakes, and have a discussion to teach them even more.

The best leaders let their people make mistakes, and treat them as learning opportunities. Making mistakes is part of the learning process, and you might agree that you've learned more from your mistakes and failures than you have from your successes.

He corrected and instructed them

After the disciples met challenges, made mistakes and came back with questions, Jesus corrected and instructed them. They went out with more confidence than before, armed with experience, knowledge and wisdom of how to do it better. This process continued over and over until they learned what Jesus wanted them to learn.

What about the people you influence? Do you spend the time necessary to correct and instruct them in an encouraging way? Do they go out with more confidence than before, or do they seem discouraged? The correcting and instructing part of the guiding process is very critical to their growth. If you're not getting the results you want, try spending more time understanding how they are getting their current results. Look for a ways to compliment them on what they're doing right, and show them how to "tweak" a few things to bring different results.

He prayed for them

Jesus spent the night praying before he went out and chose the twelve disciples. (Luke 6:12–13) How times have you stayed up all night and prayed for your family, your employees or your friends? You can dramatically increase the way you influence people by praying for them. Never underestimate the power of prayer.

The best organizations guide their customers

I was referred to a man named Jerry. He bought and sold cars at the car auction. He was so good at what he did, that he could size up a car's value within a few minutes. Just watching him buy and sell cars was fun.

He asked us many questions about the car we wanted, from price down to the smallest detail. He guided us in purchasing a car. We enjoyed the process and referred many friends to him.

Summary

Think of the people God has put in your life to be a lighthouse for. You might have a spouse or children. You may have people who work for you. You may have nieces, nephews or neighbor kids who look up to you. What would happen if you guided them according to the way Jesus did? How would that impact the way you influence them?

Guiding people the Jesus way:

- He spent time with them
- He encouraged them
- He focused on training them
- He let them make mistakes
- He lovingly corrected and instructed them
- He prayed for them

The lighthouse helps the most people when it is attracting and guiding. You are the most fulfilled when you are attracting and guiding people. If you focus your thoughts on guiding people like Jesus did, you will influence them at a whole new level. More people will give you permission to guide them, and your sphere of influence will increase.

Take-Away Formula for Guiding People

- **Spend time with them**
- **Encourage them**
- **Focus on training them**
- **Let them make mistakes**
- **Lovingly correct and instruct them**
- **Pray for them**

You are the light of the world. A city on a hill cannot be hidden. Neither do people light a lamp and put it under a bowl. Instead they put it on its stand, and it gives light to everyone in the house. In the same way, let your light shine before men, that they may see your good deeds and praise your Father in heaven.

—Matthew 5:14–16

ATTRACTS

GUIDES

KNOWS
ITS
PURPOSE

UNIQUE
CHARACTER

ROCK SOLID FOUNDATION

Chapter 7
Shining Your Light

I hope you enjoyed our journey into The Lighthouse Leadership Principle. My hope is that you discovered the secrets to growing and guiding the people in your life. Do what the principles say and you will experience more fulfillment as a leader. How do I know? Because they changed my life soon after God gave them to me.

Get started building your rock solid foundation of relationships. Figure out your right ones, and prioritize them in the right order. Spend time with God, your spouse and your children. Delight in knowing them more.

You are unique and special. Celebrate your uniqueness and just be yourself.

Discover your purpose and shine your light. God prepared you for a special work before you were born. Search with all your heart and soul, and He will reveal His plan for your life. God has big plans for you:

> *"For I know the plans I have for you,"*
> *declares the Lord, " plans to prosper you and*
> *not to harm you, plans to give you hope and a*
> *future. Then you will call upon me and come*
> *and pray to me, and I will listen to you. You*
> *will seek me and find me when you seek me*

with all your heart. I will be found by you,"
declares the Lord...

—Jeremiah 29:11

Discover the joy of attracting people the way Jesus did. He was available and present for them. He served and forgave them. They loved him for it, and couldn't get enough of him.

As you guide people the way Jesus did, you will experience more peace, joy and happiness in your life. Spend time with them, encourage them, focus on training them, lovingly correct and instruct them, and pray for them.

Most importantly, just go out there and shine your light!

You are the light of the world. A city on a hill
cannot be hidden. Neither do people light a
lamp and put it under a bowl. Instead they
put it on its stand, and it gives light to every-
one in the house. In the same way, let your
light shine before men, that they may see your
good deeds and praise your Father in heaven.

—Matthew 5:14–16

About the Author

Pete Walkey is an author, speaker, leadership coach, and President of the Lighthouse Leadership Group.

He is a creative thinker who has helped companies, associations and universities solve their greatest challenges by growing their people. His engaging, entertaining, and motivating keynotes and workshops have been captivating audiences for the past 12 years, in virtually every sector of the economy. He speaks on leadership, sales and creativity topics.

He has been paid to think of ideas for Hollywood film producers, inventors, best-selling authors, radio talk show hosts, attorneys, and high-profile money managers of the rich and famous, as well as a host of companies, associations and universities.

Among the people who have paid for his ideas are:

- Mark Victor Hansen, *Chicken Soup for the Soul*
- Famous Dave Anderson, Rainforest Café, Famous Dave's Barbecue restaurants, and George W. Bush advisor.

Pete is the author of four books, including Save It Forward. He has been featured on national radio shows. He has spent over a decade addressing audiences in the Financial Services and Insurance industries.

He graduated from Manchester College where he played baseball and has run several marathons, with his wife Jill, and his father Dan.

Pete and his wife Jill live in Indianapolis, have been married for 9 years, and have been blessed with three beautiful daughters; Kaylee, Ellie, and Kylie.

Additional Lighthouse Resources

In order to serve you in your quest to become the Lighthouse Leader you were born to be, or to bring *The Lighthouse Leadership Principle* to your organization, contact us at:

www.LighthouseLeadershipGroup.com

Or call:

317–727–5518

Additional *Lighthouse Leadership Principle* Formats:

- Keynotes
- Workshops
- Seminars
- Leadership Retreats
- Personal Coaching
- Mentoring
- Ongoing Leadership Training

CPSIA information can be obtained
at www.ICGtesting.com
Printed in the USA
FFOW04n0924121015
17625FF